ATLAS

Glen Baxter

JONATHAN CAPE
THIRTY BEDFORD SQUARE LONDON

For Jaco and Elizabeth

Also by Glen Baxter

THE FALLS TRACER
THE KHAKI
FRUITS OF THE WORLD IN DANGER
THE HANDY GUIDE TO AMAZING PEOPLE
CRANIREONS OV BOTYA
STORIES
THE WORKS
THE IMPENDING GLEAM

Many of the drawings in this book are in
private and public collections.

First published in The Netherlands 1979
by Uitgeverij De Harmonie, Amsterdam
First published in Great Britain 1982
This collection copyright © 1982 by Glen Baxter
Jonathan Cape Ltd, 30 Bedford Square, London WC1

Reprinted 1983

British Library Cataloguing in Publication Data

Baxter, Glen
Atlas.
1. English wit and humor, Pictorial
I. Title
741.5'942   NC1479
ISBN 0-224-02941-X

Printed in Great Britain by St Edmundsbury Press
Bury St Edmunds, Suffolk

CONTENTS

That Fateful Encounter

"NOW THIS MAY LOOK LIKE AN ORDINARY
NOSE....." BEGAN THE TRAVELLER

JANET HAD OPTED TO FLY "TOURIST CLASS"

THE GEOLOGIST SPENT MANY HOURS
REHEARSING THE GLOW-WORM TROUPE

THE INSURANCE SALESMAN MOVED IN
BRANDISHING HIS POLICIES

IT WAS HARVEY'S BOLD PLAN TO ARRIVE AT THE
ENEMY HEADQUARTERS AT PORT ARTHUR UNDETECTED...

IT WAS AN OFFER SHE
DARE NOT REFUSE

GREAT
FAILURES
OF OUR
TIME

No. 6   *The First Parachute*

ALEC SENSED THAT LIFE SOMEHOW
WAS PASSING HIM BY....

HE SPOKE FERVENTLY OF HIS VISION
OF A CHAIN OF MULTI-LEVEL PANCAKE
HOUSES IN EVERY MAJOR CITY IN
THE NETHERLANDS.......

TOM TRIED OUT THE NEW BULLET.....

HARRY AND HIS TRICK FINGER
WERE BEGINNING TO BECOME
TIRESOME NOTED MASSINTON.

GREAT CULINARY DISASTERS OF OUR TIME

FILETS de CANETON au CHERRY MARNIER
(pour 2 personnes), NEWPORT PAGNELL 2/3/73

STEWED FIGS AMERICAN STYLE —
ANTWERP, NOVEMBER 3RD 1974

GRATIN de LANGOUSTE à la NORMANDE,
EDINBURGH 14/8/58

CHICKEN MARYLAND, WEMBLEY 14/2/53

CAULIFLOWER POLONAISE, NEW CROSS-
SOUTH LONDON 23RD SEPTEMBER 1976

ASPARAGUS IN MUSTARD SAUCE, UTRECHT
APRIL 11TH 1949

HOT DOG ZUCCHINI COMBO, BELGRADE 2/2/68

"SPECIAL OF THE DAY", APRIL 14, 1963
CANAL STREET, NEW YORK

FEGATO ALLA VENEZIANA, DUSSELDORF, 21/11/28

CHICKEN FRIED RICE, MERTHYR
TYDFIL, SEPTEMBER 26TH 1971

THEY WERE JUST ABLE TO MAKE OUT
THE LONELY FIGURE OF THE CHIROPODIST.

"I WHITTLE THESE!" BLURTED CRAIG

"ANOTHER SLIM VOLUME OF MODERN
ENGLISH POETRY!" SHRIEKED JACOBSEN

MR BOTTOMLEY HELD VERY FIXED IDEAS
ABOUT INTERIOR DESIGN....

IT WAS PRECISELY SIX-FIFTEEN

HELMUT CHECKED THE BOULDER AT TWELVE
MINUTE INTERVALS THROUGHOUT THE NIGHT.

IT WAS MRS. CRABTREE, AND SHE
WAS IN NO MOOD FOR PLEASANTRIES

MADDOX SCRUTINIZED THE WORM'S
PROGRESS

"THESE PANTS ARE WELDED STEEL"
ANNOUNCED THE STRANGER

AS THE EVENING WORE ON
I BEGAN TO SUSPECT THAT I
WAS IN THE PRESENCE OF
A DESPERATE MAN.....

THERE, AS USUAL, WAS EDELSON, DELIVERING
HIS POST-STRUCTURALIST ANALYSIS OF THE
MODERN NOVEL TO THE PRIVILEGED FEW.

THE DEAN WASN'T THERE ANY MORE

"THAT'S L-E-P-A-G-E WITH AN
E" CORRECTED THE DOORMAN

WITH
COLONEL
BAXTER
IN THE
FOOTHILLS

IT WAS CLEARLY A PRIMITIVE
DEVICE FOR SHREDDING BEETROOT

THE DISTRICT COMMISSIONER'S MINT TEA
WAS HELD IN AWE THROUGHOUT THE FOOTHILLS.

RIDLEY WAS ROUSED EACH MORNING
AT 7·15 SHARP.

SYBIL GASPED. THERE ON N'BOTO'S
PALM WAS TATTOOED A PERFECT
STREET MAP OF DUNDEE.....

I WAS OBLIGED TO ENDURE THE
ROUTINE KNEE INSPECTION

"DIE SCHWIERIGKEIT IST, DIE
GRUNDLOSIGKEIT UNSERES
GLAUBENS EINZUSEHEN"
NOTED NGOTOGO

THERE IT WAS—THE LEGENDARY BALL
OF SOOT OF THE XOACAPOTALX

"I'LL NEVER FORGET THE DAY M'BLAWI
STUMBLED ON THE WORK OF THE
POST–IMPRESSIONISTS...."

"CAN'ST THOU NOT SEE IT, MY LIEGE? 'TIS BUT
THREE BLOCKS NORTH OF THE DELICATESSEN..."

IT WAS RUDOLPH'S TURN TO
LUBRICATE THE CINDERS

IT SEEMED TO AMUSE HIM, SO
I COMPLIED WITH HIS ODD REQUEST...

TUESDAYS, WEDNESDAYS
AND FRIDAYS...

THURSDAYS WERE
SET ASIDE FOR PLAITING

YOUNG ROSENBERG HAD PERFECTED A
METHOD OF COATING SHOELACES WITH
TWO THIN LAYERS OF UNSALTED BUTTER

IT WAS GOING TO BE
THE USUAL DULL CHRISTMAS

"BUT I <u>AM</u> THE POSTMAN!" BLURTED NTONGA

PHYLLIS REALIZED ALMOST INSTINCTIVELY
THAT IT WAS JUST A PIECE OF PAPER.

SLEEPING IN THE GUEST BEDROOM DID,
HOWEVER, HAVE ITS DRAWBACKS......

"WE'LL HAVE NO ALLITERATION IN THIS HERE BUNKHOUSE" SNORTED McCULLOCH

UNCLE ARTHUR WAS GOING THROUGH ONE OF HIS "DIFFICULT" PATCHES AGAIN

SETH'S SNOOD WAS THE ENVY
OF THE BOYS IN THE BUNKHOUSE

GREAT FAILURES
OF OUR TIME

First Dental Extraction
by Red Admiral

SPRIGG ALWAYS HAD THE SUET MAILED
FIRST CLASS FROM DRESDEN

AFTER LIGHTS OUT, SMYTHE WOULD TAP OUT A CHAPTER OF "PRIDE AND PREJUDICE" IN MORSE CODE FOR THE LADS IN DORMITORY 'K'.....

GLADYS HAD NOT REALIZED THAT VIRGINIA
WAS UNABLE TO ACCEPT DEFEAT GRACEFULLY

GREAT FAILURES OF OUR TIME

№ 226 The First Fly Swat

"IF A FACT IS TO BE A PICTURE IT MUST
HAVE SOMETHING IN COMMON WITH WHAT
IT DEPICTS" MUSED THREEVES

EAKINS SPENT MOST OF
THANKSGIVING WORKING ON
HIS OIL DRUM TECHNIQUE...

DAYS CAME AND WENT — ANXIOUS DAYS IN WHICH WINIFRED NEVER MENTIONED HER INCREDIBLE EXPEDITION TO SEE THE GENERAL.

GREAT FAILURES
OF OUR TIME

№ 23

First Transatlantic

Crossing

BEFORE PLATT COULD CROSS THE BALL,
THE BIG NUMBER FIVE LUMBERED UP
AND LASHED HIM WITH HIS QUIFF....

"CAN'T YOU SEE, BIGGS, THAT WHAT WE HAVE HERE IS ALMOST CERTAINLY EVIDENCE OF SOME PRIMITIVE FORM OF A TAKE-AWAY FOOD SERVICE......"

"TAKE A TIP FROM ME, YOUNG FELLER—
ALWAYS CARRY A SPARE GOATEE...."

IT WAS CLEARLY THE BELGIAN WHO
WAS TAMPERING WITH THE PILCHARDS

THE DRIVER GRINNED AT THE OBVIOUS TWINKLE.

" SO, YOU'VE ALMOST PERFECTED YOUR INVISIBLE RAY, EH WILKINS?"

GREAT FAILURES OF OUR TIME

Nº 224 The First Frankfurter

KEN WAS KNOWN TO GO
TO EXTREME LENGTHS IN
THE PREPARATION OF HIS
SYLLABUBS...

"MISTER.... JES KEEP YOUR
JUNGIAN ANALYSIS TO
YO'SELF.... YOU HEAR?"
GROWLED MRS BOTHAM

"THIS BEARD OF YOURS SEEMS TO BE
FASHIONED FROM CORK" SNAPPED BLY.

GREAT FAILURES
OF OUR TIME

Nº 19 The First Corkscrew

"QUITE GOOD, RUNNING ELK — YOUR WORK
ON THE APOSTROPHE IS COMING ALONG
— BUT THERE IS STILL MUCH TO LEARN..."
COMMENTED MR. THUNEGRENCH

GREAT FAILURES OF OUR TIME

Nº 242   The First Hula Hoop

"THE GAME'S UP, MRS SO-CALLED RAMSTED!"
BARKED INSPECTOR THRUMM

"THIS IS WHAT I THINK OF YOUR
WALLPAPER DESIGNS!" CROAKED
MR. LATIMER

"THAT IS MR SMOLLET'S EYEBROW!"
DECLARED JANEY

YOUNG ROBERTS COULD NOT FACE ANOTHER MOUSSAKA

EVERY OTHER WEDNESDAY THE LADS
WERE ALLOWED AN EXTRA RATION

THE NEAREST TAXIDERMIST WAS
STILL THREE DAYS' MARCH AWAY